About Mammals

For the One who created mammals.

—*Genesis* 1:24

Published by
PEACHTREE PUBLISHERS
1700 Chattahoochee Avenue
Atlanta, Georgia 30318-2112
www.peachtree-online.com

Text © 1997, 1999, 2014 by Cathryn P. Sill
Illustrations © 1997, 1999, 2014 by John C. Sill

Illustrations created in watercolor on archival quality 100% rag watercolor paper
Text and titles set in Novarese from Adobe Systems

Printed and manufactured in April 2014 by Imago in Singapore

10 9 8 7 6 5 4 3 2 1 (hardcover)
10 9 8 7 6 5 4 3 2 1 (trade paperback)
Revised Edition

Library of Congress Cataloging-in-Publication Data

Sill, Cathryn P.
  About mammals: a guide for children / Cathryn Sill; illustrated by John Sill.
  p. cm.
  Summary: Explains what mammals are, how they live, and what they do.
  ISBN 978-1-56145-757-1 (hardcover)
  ISBN 978-1-56145-758-8 (trade paperback)
  I. Mammals—Juvenile literature. [I. Mammals.] I. Sill, John, ill. II. Title.
  QL706.2.S547 1997
  500—dc20   96-36402

About Mammals

A Guide for Children

Revised Edition

Cathryn Sill

Illustrated by John Sill

PEACHTREE
ATLANTA

Mammals have hair.

PLATE 1
Northern Raccoon

They may have thick fur,

PLATE 2
Muskox

sharp quills,

PLATE 3
North American Porcupine

John Sill

or only a few stiff whiskers.

PLATE 4
Walrus

Baby mammals drink milk from their mothers.

PLATE 5
American Bison

John Sill

Some mammals are born helpless.

Others can move about on their own soon after they are born.

Mammals may run,

PLATE 8
Pronghorn

climb,

swim,

or fly.

Mammals eat meat,

PLATE 12
Bobcat

plants,

PLATE 13
American Pika

or both.

They live in cold and icy places,

hot and dry deserts,

or wet marshes.

PLATE 17
Common Muskrat

It is important to protect mammals and the places where they live.

Afterword

PLATE 1
There are more than 5,000 species of mammals in the world. About 450 different kinds live in the United States and Canada. Hair is adapted to protect mammals according to the needs of each species. The coats of the Northern Raccoon grow thicker in winter to keep them warm and dry. Northern Raccoons are found in many different habitats across much of North America.

PLATE 2
Hair protects mammals in different kinds of weather. It also helps keep the animal's skin from being injured or sunburned. Many mammals have more than one kind of hair. The hair most easily seen is called "guard hair." Beneath the guard hair is a layer called "underfur." Muskoxen have a thick outer coat of long guard hairs and a dense undercoat that keep them warm in frigid temperatures. Muskoxen live in the cold Arctic region.

PLATE 3
Some mammals have thick, stiff guard hairs on parts of their bodies. North American Porcupines have sharp quills on their backs and tails. The quills are loosely attached and will come off and stick into an enemy's body. North American Porcupines live in the northern and western parts of North America.

PLATE 4

Whiskers are a special kind of hair that helps mammals learn information about their surroundings. Some marine mammals have only a few coarse whiskers. Walruses use their sensitive, bristly whiskers to find food on the ocean floor. They eat snails, clams, crabs, and shrimp. Walruses live in the Arctic Ocean and some northern parts of the Pacific and Atlantic Oceans.

PLATE 5

Mammals get their name from the special mammary glands that make milk for their young. American Bison babies drink milk from their mothers for about seven months. American Bison (also called "American Buffalo") were nearly hunted to extinction in the late 1800s. Laws now protect them and their numbers are slowly increasing. American Bison are the largest land animals in North America. They live in central and western United States and Canada.

PLATE 6

Mother mammals usually take good care of their babies. They feed, groom, and protect them until they are able to live on their own. White-footed Deermice are born blind and hairless. Their eyes open when they are about two weeks old. The babies are weaned at around three weeks. By the time they are ten or eleven weeks old, they have grown to adult size. White-footed Deermice live throughout most of the eastern United States. They also live in parts of Canada and Mexico.

PLATE 7

Grazing mammal babies must be able to travel along as their mothers search for food. The young animals must be able to run very fast soon after birth to avoid danger from predators. Elk (also called "Wapiti") babies can stand up about twenty minutes after they are born. Elk used to be common over most of North America, but hunting caused them to disappear from eastern North America. They have been successfully reestablished in several places where they used to live.

PLATE 8

Most land mammals walk or run on all four legs. Pronghorns must be able to run fast to escape from danger since they live in open areas without many hiding places. They can run over 50 miles per hour (80 kmh) for several miles. Pronghorns are the fastest mammals in North America. They live in western and central North America.

PLATE 9

Animals that climb must be able to hold on to keep from falling. Squirrels have sharp claws that help them grasp trunks and branches and allow them to make their way easily through trees. American Red Squirrels are small, noisy tree squirrels that stay safe from predators by moving quickly. They live in forests in parts of the United States and Canada.

PLATE 10
Mammals that live in the water all of the time use their flippers to steer and their tails to push themselves as they swim. Blue Whales are the largest animals that have ever lived on Earth. They swim in all the oceans of the world.

PLATE 11
While some mammals can glide from tree to tree, bats are the only ones that truly fly. Big Brown Bats are one of the fastest bats. They can fly at speeds up to 40 miles per hour (64 kmh). Big Brown Bats eat flying insects, including beetles, moths, flies, and wasps. They live in North America, Central America, the northern part of South America, and the Caribbean Islands.

PLATE 12
Animals that eat meat are called "carnivores." Some mammals, such as wild cats, eat only meat. Although Bobcats can kill animals larger than themselves, they hunt mainly rabbits, squirrels, and mice. Bobcats live throughout most of North America.

PLATE 13

Animals that eat plants are called "herbivores." Some plant eaters store food for winter. In midsummer, American Pikas begin to gather plants and pile them into stacks to dry in the sun. They often tuck the dried plants under a rock or log to protect them from the weather. When snow covers the ground, they move through tunnels they have built to find their "haystacks." American Pikas live in the mountains of western North America.

PLATE 14

Animals that eat meat and plants are called "omnivores." Most kinds of bears are omnivores. American Black Bears will eat many different things, including roots, berries, insects, and small mammals. They are able to live in forests, swamps, and tundra. American Black Bears are the most common bear in North America. They live in Canada, the United States, and northern Mexico.

PLATE 15

Many animals migrate from cold areas when winter comes. Those that stay are protected from the cold by thick layers of fat or dense fur coats. Arctic Foxes have white winter coats that change to brown in summer. This camouflage or protective coloration allows them to hide from both predators and prey. They have fur on their paws so they can walk on ice and snow. Arctic Foxes live throughout the entire Arctic Tundra.

PLATE 16

Desert mammals have special ways of surviving in their hot, dry habitat. Black-tailed Jackrabbits have large ears that carry the heat away from their bodies. Their excellent hearing helps them avoid predators. Jackrabbits are hares, not rabbits. Hares are usually larger than rabbits and have larger back legs and feet. Jackrabbits live in central and western North America.

PLATE 17

Many mammals are able to find food and shelter in marshes or other types of wetlands. Common Muskrats build domed houses in water using marsh vegetation. Their tails, which are flattened from side to side, help guide them as they swim. Common Muskrats live in most of Canada and the United States.

PLATE 18

One of the greatest dangers to mammals and other wildlife is habitat destruction. When we protect the environment, we benefit mammals as well as whole communities of different animals by providing places where they can find space, shelter, food, and water. *Can you find the animal in this picture that is not a mammal?*

GLOSSARY

Glide—to move smoothly without effort
Graze—to feed on growing grass
Groom—to clean fur or skin
Habitat—the place where animals and plants live
Marine Mammal—a mammal that spends all or part of its life in the sea
Predator—an animal that lives by hunting and eating other animals
Prey—an animal that is hunted and eaten by a predator
Species—a group of animals or plants that are alike in many ways
Wean—to help a nursing baby learn to find other food

BIBLIOGRAPHY

BOOKS

Eyewitness Books: Mammal by Steve Parker (Dorling Kindersley)
Kaufman Focus Guides: Mammal by Nora Bowers, Rick Bowers, and Kenn Kaufman (Houghton Mifflin Company)
Peterson First Guides: Mammals by Peter Alden (Houghton Mifflin Company)

WEBSITES

http://kids.sandiegozoo.org/animals/mammals
http://www.enchantedlearning.com/subjects/mammals/
http://www.arkive.org/mammals/

ABOUT... SERIES

ISBN 978-1-56145-234-7 HC
ISBN 978-1-56145-312-2 PB

ISBN 978-1-56145-038-1 HC
ISBN 978-1-56145-364-1 PB

ISBN 978-1-56145-688-8 HC
ISBN 978-1-56145-699-4 PB

ISBN 978-1-56145-301-6 HC
ISBN 978-1-56145-405-1 PB

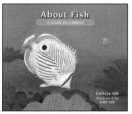

ISBN 978-1-56145-256-9 HC
ISBN 978-1-56145-335-1 PB

ISBN 978-1-56145-588-1 HC

ISBN 978-1-56145-207-1 HC
ISBN 978-1-56145-232-3 PB

ISBN 978-1-56145-757-1 HC
ISBN 978-1-56145-758-8 PB

ISBN 978-1-56145-358-0 HC
ISBN 978-1-56145-407-5 PB

ISBN 978-1-56145-331-3 HC
ISBN 978-1-56145-406-8 PB

ISBN 978-1-56145-795-3 HC

ISBN 978-1-56145-743-4 HC
ISBN 978-1-56145-741-0 PB

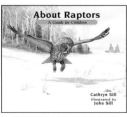

ISBN 978-1-56145-536-2 HC
ISBN 978-1-56145-811-0 PB

ISBN 978-1-56145-183-8 HC
ISBN 978-1-56145-233-0 PB

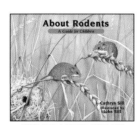

ISBN 978-1-56145-454-9 HC

ALSO AVAILABLE
IN BILINGUAL EDITION

- About Birds / Sobre los pájaros
  ISBN 978-1-56145-783-0 PB
- About Mammals / Sobre los mamíferos
  ISBN 978-1-56145-800-4 PB

ABOUT HABITATS SERIES

Deserts

ISBN 978-1-56145-641-3 HC
ISBN 978-1-56145-636-9 PB

Forests

ISBN 978-1-56145-734-2 HC

Grasslands

ISBN 978-1-56145-559-1 HC

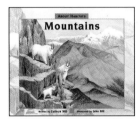

Mountains

ISBN 978-1-56145-469-3 HC
ISBN 978-1-56145-731-1 PB

Oceans

ISBN 978-1-56145-618-5 HC

Wetlands

ISBN 978-1-56145-432-7 HC
ISBN 978-1-56145-689-5 PB

THE SILLS

Cathryn Sill, a former elementary school teacher, is the author of the acclaimed ABOUT... series and the ABOUT HABITATS series. With her husband John and her brother-in-law Ben Sill, she coauthored the popular bird-guide parodies, A FIELD GUIDE TO LITTLE-KNOWN AND SELDOM-SEEN BIRDS OF NORTH AMERICA, ANOTHER FIELD GUIDE TO LITTLE-KNOWN AND SELDOM-SEEN BIRDS OF NORTH AMERICA, and BEYOND BIRDWATCHING.

John Sill is a prize-winning and widely published wildlife artist who illustrated the ABOUT... series and the ABOUT HABITATS series, and illustrated and coauthored the FIELD GUIDES and BEYOND BIRDWATCHING. A native of North Carolina, he holds a B.S. in Wildlife Biology from North Carolina State University.

The Sills live in Franklin, North Carolina.